Learn Coding

Essential Concepts for Beginners

Who Want to Start Scripting

Computer Languages

TIM WIRED

Table of Contents

Introduction

Congratulations on purchasing *Learn Programming* and thank you for doing so.

The following chapters will discuss everything that we need to work with when we are ready to work with a new programming language for the very first time. There are so many reasons why we want to work with programming and why we would consider making it our own as well. But sometimes we want to make sure that we are choosing the right language, and we want to ensure that we are set for handling some of the complexities of coding before we just right in. This is exactly how this guidebook is going to be able to help.

Inside this guidebook, we are going to take some time to not look just at one particular coding language but we are going to go back a little bit further. For some, just the idea of programming is going to be confusing, and knowing how to get started, how the languages are similar and different, and how we are able to use these for our needs is important. And we will spend some time discussing these important topics in this guidebook.

With all of the things that are present in many of the most common coding languages that are out there, and all of the options that you are able to choose from when it is time to star with your own coding project, it is no wonder why so many people are going to be worried about which language to choose, and learning some of the basics as soon as possible. And we hope that with the help of this guidebook, we will be able to get it done and help you to choose out the coding language that you would like to use.

To start with this guidebook, we are going to spend some time taking a look at the basics that come with some of the most common coding languages out there. it is going to help us learn some of the most common terms and their definitions to make it easier to really see what is going on, and to ensure that we are really prepared when it is time to enter into the world of coding.

The next thing that we need to explore is all of the main features that we are likely to see when we get started with any kind of coding language that we would like to use. We can look at some of the most common parts that we want to work with including arrays, data types, comments, and statements. While some languages will have their own special parts and some with being missing others but we will spend our time looking at some of the most common features and parts that most coding languages are going to share.

Next, it is time for us to take a look at some of the different coding languages out there, and what we are able to do with them. There are dozens of popular options, and a lot of other ones that may not be as common, but can provide us with some of the features and work that we want. We will spend some time in this chapter discussing all of the most common coding languages, what you can do with them, and some of the benefits of choosing that language over the other options that are available.

We can then move on to helping ourselves get started with some of the codings that we want to do. This chapter is going to look at the software, hardware, IDEs and more that you are able to work with along the way, with a focus on the costs being as low as possible. If you are just learning how to work with coding, or you have a big project you plan to do later with that coding that may be more expensive, finding the right tools that you can use, the ones that will provide you with the power and more that we want, for an affordable cost, is going to be important.

With this same note, we are going to spend some time looking at the different resources that you are able to use to make things easier. This is going to include some of the games you can play to learn more, the forums and communities you wan to work with, and so much more. Along with this same idea, we will spend some time in the sixth chapter looking at some of the tips and tricks that we want to look at that will make our coding strong than ever before.

To finish off this guidebook, we are going to spend some time looking at some of the steps that need to be taken in order to make sure that you pick out the right coding language for your needs. This is often one of the hardest parts that come with working on a programming option because there are so many and you want to make sure that you pick out the one that will be able to get the work done that you would like, that is going to meet your needs, and will not be too hard to work with. This chapter will ensure that you are able to figure out the best language for your needs.

Learning how to code can be an exciting experience, one that can open up a lot of doors to you, and will ensure that you are really able to reach your goals, get that application done, and even to ensure that you can get that job that you have always wanted. Taking the time to learn some of the basics that we are going to discuss in this guidebook, and really learning how to do some of the codings that you need. When you are ready to learn some of the basics that are needed when it is time to work with coding, and you want to see how successful you can be as a beginner, make sure to check out this guidebook to help you get started.

There are plenty of books on this subject on the market, thanks again for choosing this one! Every effort was made to ensure it is full of as much useful information as possible, please enjoy it!

Chapter 1: Knowing the Basics

When we talk about the word coding, we will quickly see that it is a vast and big world to look at. It is not going to include just one or two parts. It is going to include hundreds of languages, thousands of software programs, and so much more. For example, all of the software that you are going to use on your desktop and laptop, and even the games and the apps that you enjoy on your smartphone are all going to be products of this coding. Even if you are working with a gadget or a device that does not have a screen, such as an RC drone, or even the toy Furby, you will not be able to behave in the proper manner without some of the software that coders have been able to develop.

That is why we are going to get started on some of the different parts that are going to show up when it is time to work with the idea of coding and programming. No matter what kind of coding or programming language you are looking to get into, there are always a bunch of options, and figuring out how they all work, and the basics that they will all share, can make a difference in the amount of success you are going to see.

Common Programming Terms

The first thing that we need to explore inside this guidebook is some of the most common terms and the definitions that go with them in programming. No matter what kind of programming you would like to do, or the coding language that you want to choose, knowing these basics can be important. Some of the terms that you need to know to get started will include:

Program and code

Code is going to refer to the set of instructions that you can write out for the computer, or your compiler, to follow. As soon as you made a new code on a computer, and you wrote it out in a manner that the computer can process from the beginning all the way to the end without an error, you can already compile it into the program that you want.

Each programming language is going to come with its own rules when it comes to how the code should be written, and how you will work with each part of the program. Just know for now that the code is going to be the instructions that you are able to send through to the compiler, telling it how you want that program to behave.

Algorithms

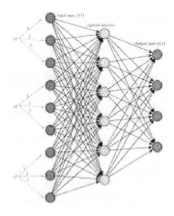

Even as a beginner, it is a good idea for you to learn a bit more about flowcharts and algorithms, even before you get really into some of the other complex stuff. When people code, they are working on providing a good solution to a problem, and they have to do this in a manner that the computer is able to understand. But if you spend too much of your time trying to craft each line of code without having a clear objective, you may find that you also have to spend a lot of time editing the code when you find out that the solution you came up with did not really address the problem, or at least not all of the situations of the problem.

Remember here that programs can be really complex to work with. According to Wired, in 2015, all of the services that Google provided over the internet were powered by 2 billion lines of code. Even some of the easier and more simple options that we would see with code, like the Windows 10 Calculator, comes with over 35,000 lines of code. Even with all of this coding, we have to remember that we can't get through all of this or make it work well if we don't go through with a game plan right from the beginning, and this is where the algorithms are going to come in to help.

The neat thing that you will notice about these algorithms is that you can do some work with them, even if you are not familiar with coding in the first place. You don't even need to work with a computer, though this does add an element of ease to the process. An algorithm is similar to what we are going to find with the code we talked about before, but it is going to be done in a manner that humans, not just the computer can understand, and it helps to give us a game plan of how to handle some of the more complex types of codes that we are going to work with.

Flowcharts

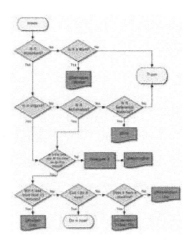

If this works, there should be some cookies that will come to your chosen website. You can then use the cookies that you have collected. You are able to use the information from the cookies, which should be saved to the website of your choice, for whatever purpose you need.

A good way for us to think about these flowcharts is as a graphical representation of an algorithm. Since these algorithms are simply just a translation of code into a human-friendly manner, a flowchart is going to provide us with more of a bird's eye view of the functionality of the code from start to finish. If you have ever done or even seen a flowchart to help see how the workflow should go, you will find that the flowcharts for coding work in a similar manner.

Flowcharting is useful in many cases because it is going to help us to make some of the more complicated programs that we need to handle significantly easier to understand. And it helps us to illustrate these complicated programs before we proceed through the coding, ensuring that we find the flaws that we want, and can make it so that we see additional features where they need to be. However, as a beginner, the best place to start is to learn about the five flowchart symbols that are going to be used in any coding flowchart that you want to work with. These are going to include:

1. Oval (Start and End): The oval, or the ellipse, is going to be a symbol that will tell us the beginning and the end of the flow of the program. To make the flowchart stay as simple as we can, you need to only use two of these ovals one for the beginning and one for the end. You can go with more than this though if your program is designed to have more than one ending though.

2. Arrow: This is going to be the line that we are able to use to help connect the shapes of your flowchart together with the arrowhead being used to tell us which direction the flow of the program is going. This is used to help eliminate the need for putting in numbered steps like you need to do when making one of the algorithms from before. Arrows add in some flexibility to the low of your

chart and can cut down on some of the clutter when the program is more complicated.

3. Parallelogram (Input and Output): This is going to help us to see the operation for the input or the output. Whenever you would like to accept a value from the user which is the input, or you would like to display a value, which is the output, in your program, make sure that the parallelogram shows up.

4. Rectangle (the process): This is going to help us to see any operation that is performed internally by the computer. Basically, any operation that is direct that doesn't accept input or doesn't display an output needs to be represented with this rectangle. For example, calculations similar to the modular division can use this kind of symbol.

5. Rhombus (Decision): This is going to be a symbol that will be used to help branch out the flow of the program or help out when handling conditional statements. It is still going to count as a process because the computer will internally do the operation, but it has to decide and then pick out the right path based on the condition that you set.

These symbols are going to be recognized universally by programmers and others who do coding, so make sure that when you are using one of these charts, you are also working with the right symbols along the way.

Programmers, coders, and developers

It is impossible for us to get very far in some of the work that we want to do with coding without taking the time to mention programming and software development. When we go from the perspective of someone who has some basic knowledge of these things, it may seem like the ideas of developing, programming, coding, and computing are all going to be the same, and can be used in a manner that is interchangeable.

However, it is important to note that those who spend a lot of time coding and work with this on a more technical level will actually know that developers, coders, and programmers are going to be very different things. A good way to think about them is like they are ranks. The coder is going to be the starter, or the most basic, level, and then to programmers and ending with the developers.

The role of a coder is going to stay pretty basic as we go through the process. You will set, or be given, a problem or an objective that you would like to achieve, and then you can utilize your knowledge in the coding language of your choice to get the job all done. Once you have been able to learn some of the basics of the chosen coding language and start pumping out the codes, and these actually work, then you would be considered a coder.

But there are some other levels as well. Programmers are going to know that coding is nothing more than just a phase of the development process for new software, one that may never end. Spending a lot of time improving the flowcharts and the algorithms that we talked about before are important parts of a good programmer. Coders are going to specialize in being able to translate some of the algorithms to code, but the programmers are going to spend time making sure they can make the algorithm even better and will check for any big bugs that could ruin the program.

We can then finish up with a developer. This is going to add another level to what we are going to see with some of the codings that happen. Developers are going to be seen more like the real brains behind the program, and they will do as much work as necessary, and as much research, to make solid flowcharts and algorithms. They will identify a target market and all of the potential problems that they have to address with a bunch of solutions.

It is also possible that these developers are going to manage a team of programmers to handle some of the bigger projects and to make sure that no matter what the vision of the developer is, the work meets that expectation. These are going to be the people who know the most about coding and programming and will make sure that the codes that are written for those programs are high level and will work properly.

Programming language

The compiler is going to understand the instructions that you are sending over, only if you speak the right language. You have to know ahead of time what the programming language of the computer is before you can provide the commands and the instructions that you need here. The good news is that you are able to make your computer smart by installing a variety of programs that will help the machine to understand as many programming languages as you want. We will spend some time later in this guidebook learning about some of the most common languages and what we are able to do with them.

Source Code Editor

This kind of editor is going to be a special kind of text editor that has been designed in a manner to aid coders in writing out some of the codes they want. You are free to enter, make, and even edit the source code, no matter what language, with the help of a basic text editor like the TextEdit for Mac OS and the Windows Notepad, and then provide the right extension of the file depending on the programming language that we are working with.

However, we have to know that some of the normal text editors are going to lack some of the features that you would like to find in the source-code editors. For example, you will not be able to find out whether something is wrong with your code. Microsoft Word is set up to help us figure out whether there is some bad spelling or bad grammar in a similar manner to a source-code editor is able to foresee if the code you wrote out is going to provide you an error.

Keep in mind that the more complication and power that is in your code, the harder it is to debug, edit, and improve the code that you have. The source code editor is going to help us out with this as well because it can automatically indent the right spots to help you see the different sections of the program, and highlight the elements and will help us to see more of the code as well. Picking out the right editor is going to be important to ensure that you are able to get them to work as well as possible.

The interpreter and compiler

The interpreter and compiler are going to come with different approaches when it is time to translate your code. The compiler is going to work by taking the entire source code, making the translations that are needed, and then outputting the program in an executable program. This process can take a bit of time based on the processor or CPU speed that you are working with, and how many lines of code are in the program. Depending on the programming language or the compiler you decide to use, this process can even complete itself well even when you find that the code has some critical errors and bugs in the code.

However, this is where we are going to find the interpreter to be useful. Rather than having to take on the entire code of source, and building a translated output, the interpreter compiles the first line of code and when each of the translations is done, the statement is going to be executed. The interpreter is then going to move on to the following line and will repeat this process until the operation is over, or until it finds an error.

Because the compiling and the executing process is going to happen on each line, the program is going to go through its execution at a slower rate, and it can be something that is more noticeable if you work with a slower CPU. But the advantage of working with this is that you will not have to wait for the whole program to compile before you can do the testing and many come with an interface that will help you figure out where the main problem is.

The debugger

The next thing that we need to take a look at is the debugger. This is going to be an external program that is designed in order to detect bugs and errors that show up in our programs and code. It is going to have some of the same functions of an interpreter, but it often has some extra functionality that comes with it, such as the ability to pause some of your operations if the command might be correct in the sense of the syntax, but will produce the wrong output.

The above example is still going to be seen as a bug because it is not an output that is undesirable, so the debugger is going to stop you there and will allow you some time to correct the code and see the operation continue if the problem is solved. Some of the debuggers that you work with may have a virtual environment that you can work with that allows you to fully check out the length and complicated code without needing to worry about compiling in the first place.

IDE

The IDE is going to be a basic kind of source code editor, but with the IDE, or the integrated development environment, you are going to be placed into the sandbox with a bucket along with all of the tools that you have to use in order to build up some serious codes right away. You will generally have all of the things that you need to get things done so that you are able to get the code done.

Most of the modern IDE's that you want to work with will be friendly to work with and will include the debuggers, interpreters, and more. Some of these are going to be able to help support more than one programming language here. You are able to choose the kind of IDE that you would like to work in order to get the results that you want.

The Library

It is always a lot more efficient for us to handle parts of our code in the library rather than in the program proper. Libraries are not only going to help us to sort out some of the different components of a program that may be more complicated, but they are going to make things easier in coding other programs. Maybe two of the programs that you are working with will have some similarities when it comes to the coding that you are doing, and because of this, you will find that it is more efficient to code with the same library. This helps you to not have to repeat yourself when you build each one from the ground up. When you are able to implement some of the libraries that are the most widely used in your code, you will get more tools that you can work with and you will not have to build them up from scratch.

Framework

Depending on the program that you would like to make, not all people will like to work with the IDE that we talked about before. Even if you do come with all of the tools and libraries within reach and the algorithms planned out, you will find that getting started on some of the coding projects that you have more of a challenge.

A framework is one method that you are able to use in order to handle this issue. A framework is basically going to be a collection of libraries that are related and can help us to reduce how much code is necessary to achieve some of the goals that we have. there are a lot of frameworks that you are able to work with and they support all kinds of languages based on what you want to do.

As we can see here, there are a lot of different terms and definitions that we need to know in order to get started with some of the codings that we would like to accomplish. Having a good understanding of how these are supposed to work and what we are able to do with them is going to really matter when it is time to work on the codes that we would like.

Hopefully, this has provided us with some of the introduction that we are looking for, and we will be able to use this to help us learn more about coding and to see that the information is really all that hard and scary like we may have thought in the past. Programming can be simple too, and sometimes the toughness that comes with it is going to be more in our head than anything else.

Chapter 2: Common Features Coding Languages Share

Some of the beauty of coding is the fact that there are a lot of coding languages that you are able to work with. Sometimes it is going to seem chaotic because each of these languages works on different things and they will have their benefits and negatives to consider. Some are going to be a bit easier to work with and some are harder. And each of them works with a lot of different types of programming that you want to work with.

The good news here is that no matter which of the programming languages you want to work with, you will need to know a bit about some of the common features and components that the languages are going to share with one another. Some of the parts that we are able to remember here will be:

The statements

Here, we can see an example of the If loop implementation with and Else statements.

Listing 1: If loop with Else If and Else

```
1 If [cond] Then
2     [code]
3 ElseIf [cond] Then
4     [code]
5 Else
6     [code]
7 End If
```

Each line of the code that you are going to work with will be known as a statement. Sometimes these are long and you will need to break them up to make it work, and sometimes they are going to be a little bit longer. Sometimes the programming language is going to ask you to have a special character at the end, usually a semicolon, to help denote that the command is done at that time.

You are able to make these statements into anything that you would like. They can be a short sentence or a whole explanation of what you would like to see happen in some of the codings that you would like to do. It will not take long of working with some of the coding languages out there before you start to notice how prevalent these statements really can be for your coding.

The Comment

```
void foo()
{
    for (int i=0 ; i<VALUES_SIZE ; i++)
    {
        int x=i*2;//does very long comments about all
        code in this line
        int y=i*2;//above really very very very very long
        comments about actual code in this long line
        spreading over too as three long lines
    }
}
```

Comments are another tool that we are able to use when it comes to coding. You are able to add in these comments in order to describe what is going on at a certain part of the code and leave yourself, or another programmer, a little message as to what is going on in some of the code that you are writing along the way as well. You can add in a lot of these comments into your code if you would like, but keeping it to a minimum is important to ensure that the process is going to continue working.

Each language is going to have a special symbol that you will need to put in front of the comment that you are writing to ensure the compiler knows that this is a comment. If you use the right symbol, the compiler will know to skip over this statement, and will not try to execute it or ruin your code.

A good example of this is the Python language. If you would like to write out a comment inside of this language, you would simply add the # symbol ahead of time. if the comment is going to take up more than a few lines of code, then you would be able to add that symbol before each line of code that you are working with as well. While other coding languages are going to use a different kind of symbol to get the work done, you will find that this can really be a similar matter with each of them, and you will be able to make this work to add in as many comments as you would like.

The Syntax

The syntax is basically the rules of how you are able to write out a specific part of the code. Each code is going to have syntax based on how the compiler will be able to read through the information. The syntax is often like the grammar rules that we have to follow in our own language, but it is more direct to the point and usually has rules that are stricter. You have to learn the programming language rules and do some practice to really learn how the syntax is supposed to work in some of the codes that you are working with.

The syntax is going to be the rules that we have to follow. If you miss out on some part of the syntax that is really needed in order to handle some of the codings that you are doing, then the compiler is not going to be certain about what is there, and what you would like it to do, and it will not complete the process at all. You will most likely get an error message that shows up with this one, and then you will find that you have to go through and make some of the changes as well.

Now, one of the first things that you should focus on when it is time to work in any coding language, its syntax. You should be able to catch on to some of these along the way pretty quickly, but it is still important to make this a big priority for some of the work that you are doing and to ensure that your code is going to work the way that you would like. Take some time to learn more about this syntax and how it is going to work for your needs, and it will help move you forward more with any of the coding languages that you choose to work with along the way.

The data type

For most coding languages, you will find that data is going to be important. You get to choose what kind of data you would like to assign to your variable depending on the inputs that you are expecting form the user. The variable is going to be a reserved space on the memory of your computer to store that value later on. Picking the right one is going to provide us with a good balance between making sure the outputs we have are not unwanted and maintaining the optimal amount of performance.

Data is so important when you are learning how to code along the way. and you want to make sure that you are taking care of the data types, and learning what each of them is. They will all have an important role when it comes to the work that they are able to do inside of your code, so take your time, learn how these are meant to work, and then stick it out until you are able to make it work for some of your needs as well.

For example, you may notice that there are a lot of data types like the lists, the dictionaries, the integers, and floating numbers, the tuples, and more. All of these are going to hold onto different parts of the coding language and will help you to get things done, but you will use them in various situations based on what is working for you, and what you would like to accomplish in that part as well.

Each of the coding languages that you decide to spend your time on will have these data types and will spend time teaching you how to make them work. Spend some special time on these because they really can make or break some of the programs that you are trying to write out, and while there are many similarities that you will see with the data types in each language some languages will have unique types of data and it is important to work with these as well.

```
>>> A = np.array([[1,2,3],[4,5,6]])
>>> out = np.array([[True, False, True],[False, Tru
>>>
>>> B = A
>>>
>>> B[out] = A[out]+1
>>>
>>> B
array([[2, 2, 4],
       [4, 6, 6]])
>>> A
array([[2, 2, 4],
       [4, 6, 6]])
```

Variables and constants

These should be easy to learn more about. The constant is going to be a value that you place into your program, but it is not meant to change. You are going to assign a fixed value to a special name tag so that you are able to reference back to it in the future. Then there are the variables that the ones that are going to change to something else that comes with that type of data.

Another thing to note here is that the act of defining the variable or the data type of a constant is going to be known as the declaration. But the act of setting a value to your constant or variable for the first time is going to be initialization. Just keep in mind that this declaration isn't going to be necessary for each programming language so you have to look at the documentation of that chosen language.

A good thing to remember with these variables is what they entail. They are going to hold onto a specific spot in the memory of your computer. If you just put a variable up in the code though, you are basically just reserving a blank spot in that memory, we have to add in value to the variable to ensure that the spot is reserved for something important.

Assigning a value over to the variable that we want to work with is going to be a simple process. In the coding languages that you can choose from, taking the equal sign and placing it between the variable and the value is going to be all that it takes. This tells the compiler that the specific value that you place with the variable needs to go into that specific spot in the memory of the computer that you reserved with the variable. You can then go through and pull it out, by calling up the variable, when it is time to run the program later on.

The arrays

Arrays are also not going to be for beginner coders, but when they are used in the proper manner, you will find that they make the program more efficient. If you find that you are spending too much time making a lot of variables to store data that is similar, then you may find that you can simplify it all by working on an array that is going to store these values in their own cells. This can help to keep things organized a little bit more and will ensure that you are getting everything in one place.

These arrays may sound complicated but you will find that they are used quite a bit in some of the codes that you will want to write, so we do need to spend a little bit of time on them. To start with, we will find that an array is going to be one of the structures of data that you are able to use. It is going to contain a group of elements of your choice. For the most part, you will find that these elements are going to be the same type of data, such as all being strings or all being integers.

Arrays are going to show up in some of the computer programmings that we want to use because they are good at organizing some of the data that we want to use along the way. This can be done so that the related set of values is sorted through and searched in the right manner.

For example, if we are using a search engine we may be able to find an example of an array there to help store the web pages that were found in any of the searches that the user was able to perform. When it comes to displaying the necessary results then, the program is going to output one element of that specific ray at a time.

The method at which this is going to be done is going to depend on what we have set it up to do. For example, this could be done for a specified number of values, or just until all of the values that are stored in that particular array are shown in the output. While it is possible that this kind of program could go through and create a new variable for all of the results that are found, storing the results inside of the array is going to help provide us with the most efficient manner to help manage the memory that we have.

Functions, parameters, classes, and objects

```
                            Python 2.7

   1
   2   class University():
   3       def __init__(self, name, rank):
   4           self.name = name
   5           self.rank = rank
   6
   7       def name(self):
   8           print "The University name is %s" % (name
   9           print "This University is ranked at %s" %
  10
  11
  12   users = University("University of America", "#1")
  13   users.name()

                            Edit code
```

Now we are going to get into a few different parts of coding that are all going to fit together but will need to be discussed as well. Classes, functions, and objects are going to be very common in a lot of the programming languages that you want to work with. They are mainly for programmers who are more experienced, but you will find that they are important parts that come with many of the codes that you want to write.

Objects are going to play a big role in reducing how much code is necessary to handle things because they are there to help you reuse code throughout the program. Within that object, you will be able to find a collection of variables and constants that are related to one another. When you are better at creating these objects and you start to make objects that can relate to one another, you will find that your code becomes even more organized when you combine all of those objects into the same class.

A good way to think about these classes is like a glorified type of data. Rather than saving some space in the memory for one value, you are going to set aside memory for a lot of related objects and it is up to you on how you would like to define it all. Ideally, the programmer is going to use the related objects to make it easier to handle the bugs and to troubleshoot when it is necessary.

Just like what we see with the classes and objects above, functions will help us to avoid repeating the statements in more than one area of the code. You can also add in some dynamic interaction to the function, with the help of the parameters if you would like to make the function perform in different manners. Parameters are helpful because they are going to inject a lot of value into the function so that you are able to produce a new output when the code is recycled.

Conditionals

Remember when we were talking about the diamond shape that is found in our flowchart from earlier? When this is translated into the code, we will call it our conditional. Every one of our modern coding languages right now has these and it can show up many times because programs have to go through and make decisions based on the input of the user. If the user inputs this, then A is going to happen. If they input another thing, then they will see B happen.

When we are talking about computer programming, the conditional is going to be the conditional statements, and sometimes known as the decision control statements as well. These are going to be important because they are going to help us to perform a wide variety of computations or actions, and often this will be dependent on whether the programmer went through and specified a Boolean condition and this evaluates as true or false.

Apart from the case of what is known as a branch predication, this is always going to be something that we are able to achieve when we selectively alter the control flow that is there, based on one of the conditions that we decide to set from the beginning.

When we look at this from the point of view of imperative programming languages, we will find that the conditional statement is the one that we will use in most cases. But when we are working with something that is known as functional programming instead, then we are going to see a term like a conditional construct or a conditional expression will be the one used. This is because all of the terms are going to come in with their own distinct meanings, and we have to be able to recognize these and learn what they are able to do.

There are a lot of different options that we are able to see when it comes to these kinds of conditional statements. The if, the if else, and the elif is going to be some of the more common options. When you get started on one of the programming languages that you would like to use along the way, you will quickly find that there are many conditional statements, and you will be able to learn the syntax and some of the basic coding that will come with each of these for some of your own needs as well.

Operators and Operands

These are the parts of the code that will be used in the conditions and statements that you have and can help us to manipulate some of the data that we have. the stored values that are found in our constants and variables are going to be the operands we are looking for, and then the operators are going to be some of the symbols for the manipulation like + or -.

Null

When we are working with one of our conditional statements, you will basically spend time evaluating the conditions of the two values that are stored. But if you would like to make a condition that will lead to a particular statement if the stored value has nothing, then you are working with the null value. In programming, the null is going to mean, literally, nothing, but it will be different than a blank space or a zero in the program. The term or the representation of a null value is going to depend on the kind of programming language that we are working with.

Boolean

The Boolean is going to be an extension of conditions that are not needed when it is time to take a look at the evaluation of more than one condition. It is going to rely on a few operators, mainly NOT, OR< AND, and a few others. The idea with this one is to make sure that the computer is able to make some decisions based on the conditions that you set and seeing if the input is true or false based on those conditions.

When we are talking about a Boolean data type in computer science, then we are going to be talking about a type of data that is either going to be true or false in value, or one that is going to be yes or no. Sometimes it can even be on or off, or 1 or 0 based on what kind of program you are going to work on along the way and what you hope to see.

With the default of this, the Boolean data type is going to be set to be false. But there are some programming languages, though not many, that is not going to have this kind of data type. One option here is going to be the Perl language. However, when using If in the Perl language, it is going to return to us either a true or false option as well.

When we work with this kind of type of data in programming, a Boolean can sometimes be used more as a conditional statement that we talked about above, including those if statements. A good example of how this is going to work in the Perl language will include the following:

```perl
use strict;
my ($name, $password);
print "\nName: ";
chomp($name = <STDIN>);
print "\nPassword: ";
chomp($password = <STDIN>);
if (($name eq "bob") && ($password eq "example"))
{
print "Success\n"; }
else {
print "Fail\n";
die;
}
```

The Loop

A loop is basically going to be a series of statements that are held inside of a container that the programmer is able to define and it will start out with a condition. As long as we see that the condition is not met, the statement that is inside of this container is going to continue to execute over and over, until that condition is met. You can set up any kind of loop that you would like to handle some of the codes that are going on.

These loops are soon going to become some of your best friends. You will find that when we work with this option, and when we learn how to use them in the right spots, you will be able to really get a lot done. These loops can take lots of lines of codes, potentially hundreds, and can turn it into just a few lines of code overall. When you do this, it saves a lot of time and hassle, and can still have all of the power that we are looking for.

Each programming language is going to have a few different types of loops that you are able to work with. You have to make sure that you are learning when each of these is going to be used, why they are important, and how they will be able to help out with some of your own coding needs. When you are able to do this, you will find that working within this kind of language can be simple and easy as well.

Coding languages are going to include a lot of different parts in them, and often this can seem like a complicated thing to work with. When we take the time to learn these basics, no matter what kind of coding language we are working with, we will find that we are able to get the most out of some of the programming that we are trying to do.

Chapter 3: The Most Popular Coding Languages

Choosing a good programming language to work with is going to be one of the easiest and best ways for you to get started with some real coding. But if you ask any of the programmers you have worked with in the past, they are going to all recommend a different option when it comes to the language that they prefer. And with all of these opinions, you may be left scratching your head a bit. The answer that you need to figure out what the best programming language is will end up being subjective here because each programmer is going to have their own preference and their own idea of what is going to work.

For some beginners, being introduced to one of the coding languages over another could be a complete accident. Perhaps they were working with a website that had a theme from WordPress, and in the process, they ended up learning more about PHP. Perhaps they took some time to work with coding as a child when they did a Scratch program in school and this was what it took to inspire them to learn more about other kinds of languages.

With this in mind, we are going to take some time in this guidebook learning a bit more about the different types of coding languages and what we are able to do with them. We are going to look at the best ones that you are able to work with, how each of these will work, and how some are similar and some are completely different. So, let's dive in and see how each one of these is going to work.

A Look at the Popular Programming Languages

If you take a moment to do some Googling, you will find that there are dozens, if not more, programming languages that we are able to work with. Some of these are going to be beloved and you will find a lot of coders out will love working with this. Some are going to be hated by programmers, some are going to be obsolete. And sometimes there are new ones that are being developed to meet a need in this field.

The number of programming language types that you are able to work with can also depend on who you ask, and even which guidebook you choose to work with. To make this as easy as possible, we are going to take a look at the three main classification types of programming languages that we should know more about. These will include:

1. Image languages: These are going to be the languages that have been stripped down quite a bit. This allows us to learn about some of the concepts of programming with the help of manipulating various images along the way.

2. Block languages: These kinds of languages are often going to be known as bubble languages as well. These kinds of programming languages are going to allow the users to go through and snap together parts of code, rather than writing out the code themselves. This is going to be a visual as image languages are going to give you a look at the actual code, so you see what is happening, but you will not have to physically type it out for yourself.

3. The real programming languages: These are some of the more traditional coding languages that you are able to work with, the ones where you will actually have to go through and type things out line by line. you will find that some languages like Java, Lua, PHP JavaScript, and Python are going to fit into this.

You have to remember here that the coding language that you decide to go with should not be based on your own age. You can find that there are kids who are ready to jump in and start working with the Java language right away, especially if they would like to do some work with Minecraft at an early age. And then there are adults who want to work with some of the block-based tools if they find that learning in a visual manner rather than a text-based model is the best option for you.

But one thing that we have to consider when picking out the language is that no matter which of the many great programming languages that you choose, the one that you start with should be based on the comfort level that you have. you should not push any of your coding skills, especially as a beginner, and learn how to believe in a more natural progression along the way.

With that said, let's take a look at some of the most common coding languages that you are able to work with, and some of the things that you are able to do with each one. This can give us a good idea of how these languages are meant to work, and what we will be able to do with them along the way.

HTML and CSS

HTML, which is known as Hypertext Markup Language, and the CSS, which is known as the Cascading Style Sheets, are going to be two of the most important technologies that you will be able to learn about when it is time to create some of the web pages that you want. HTML is going to help make sure that the web page you are on will have the right structure, which could be everything from the images, the tables, lists, headings, hyperlinks, sound, videos, and any of the other elements that you would like to add into the page, as long as you label them in the right manner inside of the code.

Then the HTML is going to be the language that will work in the right way to help the web browser that we work with understand the elements that we have been able to create, and will then display some of the files of the website in the proper manner as well.

Then we can move on to the CSS language. This is going to be the one that we need to use with the HTML because it is going to be able to change up the way that the HTML looks, which the user is able to edit to customize the fonts, layouts, colors, and the presentation. This will ensure that the presentation of that website is going to look right, no matter what kind of device you are using, or the size of the screen that you are relying on.

One of the biggest things that we are going to see with CSS and how it can help us to is laid out all of our images, elements, CSS styling, and other pieces that we want to put on our page. While HTML and CSS are languages that are going to be used together in many cases, it is possible to see these two languages work independently of one another. In fact, it is this independence that makes it possible for users to share the style sheets, even with a page that is not HTML, or with any XML based kind of language.

For either of these two languages to work, you will need to have a few things in place. This includes a web browser, which can be any of the modern web browsers that you would like, and any of the simple text editors out there that can help you to save some of the files that you decide to create during this time.

If you are looking to work with any kind of web development that is out there, you may find that tinkering a bit with the HTML language is one of the best options that you are able to work with. It can at least be something good that you can spend your time on and learn more about in case you ever need to work with some of the web pages for personal or business use. On the other hand, some people find that they like to go more with the design of a web page, and then they are going to prefer going with the CSS instead.

PHP

The second language that we are going to take a look at is going to be the PHP language, which stands for Hypertext Preprocessors. This is going to be a server-side, open-source scripting language, which is going to be used along with CSS and HTML together to handle some of the task automation that you want to work with. PHP allows us to really work with incorporating some of the advanced features that we want to have with our website, such as having a shopping cart for online stores, forums, and some of the bigger and more complex image galleries that you need, among others.

When you are working with PHP, you will also be able to create a lot of apps that can be sued on your websites, such as a unit converter, a to-do list, an RSS reader and more. It is also pretty easy for us to go through and embed the PHP that we need int the HTML code, so that we can easily connect to some of the various databases that we want to pull information from, such as Oracle and MySQL>

The main difference that you are going to see with HTML and PHP is where the scripting is going to be accomplished. The HTML code is going to be done more on the browser of the user, which means on the client-side of things, and then the PHP coding will be done on the server, right before it actually goes live on the browser of the user.

There are going to be a few things that we need to have in place when we want to work with some of the PHP code. To start, we need to make sure that we have just a little bit of knowledge about HTML. You will also need any of these two requirements below:

1. A web host that is able to support the PHP language.
2. PHP and a web server that is installed on your computer. You are able to find many of these online for free to work with.

In addition to some of this, we will find that there are a few different rules for PHP that we need to know how to work with as well. To start:

1. You will need to write out the codes that you need in PHP on notepads, and then you can save them with the extension of .php in the end.
2. You should not work with something like a Word Processor because these are not going to handle some of the things that you want in your code as well as you would like. Instead, it is better to stick with the notepad instead.
3. Like HTML, the PHP syntax is going to work with opening and closing tags to help the compiler to know where all of the different parts are.

4. The whitespace that shows up is not going to be that big deal with the syntax of PHP.

5. HTML can be included within the PHP files, and they are going to work, but you will not be able to do this the other way.

As you can see from the example above that you can customize a webpage with whatever smaller projects that you can with the PHP syntax and then incorporate the elements of HTML to help organize the entire web page to work the way that you want.

You will find that working with the PHP language is going to be one of the most widely used server-side languages that you can work with, even if there are other languages that can compete and will be better at the work and more efficient at it as well. In fact, there are many programmers who would argue that PHP isn't going to be all that secure or even nice to work with, but you will find that this is a language that has seen a lot of improvements since it was first started. And the newer versions of this have become powerful tools when you would like to create some web pages that are more interactive and dynamic than ever before.

JavaScript

The JavaScript Language

The next kind of language on our list that we need to spend some time on is the JavaScript language. This one is really popular. In fact, according to a StackOverflow survey that was done in 2018, JavaScript is used by about 62.5 percent of the respondents at that time.

This is a language that was originally created back in 1995 and it was meant to be a solution for the compatibility issues that plagued the internet in some of its earlier years. But since that time, it has been used to expand beyond some of the things that we can do with the development of websites and even some of the web-based applications. Now we are able to use it on some of the more modern technologies that are available to us today such as servers, robotics, apps on our phones and more.

If you spend time liking things on Instagram or Facebook, or you have ever filled out a form on a website, then it is likely that the code that was behind all of this, and the code that will ensure that this task actually works is going to involve at least a little bit of the JavaScript language. You will find that to make this work better, it is a good idea to have some comfort with working on a few other coding languages like PHP, CSS, and HTML as well.

If you have spent some time on the CSS and HTML languages that we talked about before and have used these as techniques to master some of your own skills in web development, then you will find that the JavaScript language is going to be one of the next logical languages for you to learn how to use. This is because the JavaScript language is going to be responsible for the behavior that we will be able to see on that website. A good example of this is that JavaScript is able to tell us if there is some kind of error when we are filling out a form and if one of the fields is not handled properly.

JavaScript is also going to be used in other locations outside of web browsers. We can easily see that it is going to be found in places like various types of hardware, software, and mobile apps. This is why it has really changed to become more of a general-purpose language than it was in the past.

CoffeeScript

This one may not be known as much as some of the other options that are out there, but it is still an option that we need to spend some of our time on nonetheless. This language is going to handle some of the work that we do in a slightly different manner than some of the other coding languages that are on the list. Rather than going through and compiling the code that we are using in a manner that is readable to a human and then switching it over to the machine-readable code, this language is going to compile the code to work in JavaScript.

This kind of language is going to be there for the programmers who would like to code in JavaScript, but who do not like all of the rules and the syntax that is there. it is easier to work with because you will not have to write out as much code in the process compared to what is there in JavaScript. A good way to think about this language is that it is going to have a combination of some of the benefits that we see with Python and Ruby, while still giving us the end result that we would get with JavaScript.

This is going to make the runtime debugging that we need to do a little more of a challenge overall. But you will find that there are a lot of online resources that are available to handle this, and many of the games and interactive code editors are going to be able to support this, serving as a little proof that this language is going to exist for those who are going to have a headache with learning how to code in the traditional JavaScript language.

SQL

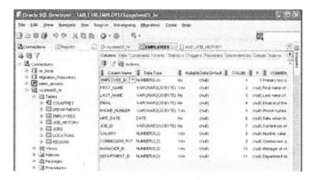

The next language that is on our list is going to be known as SQL, or Structured Query Language. This is going to be a language that is able to communicate back to a relational database system. SQL queries are going to refer to some of the statements that are going to be used in this particular language. These statements are able to do a wide variety of things for us and can work on a lot of different tasks including:

1. UPDATE: This one is going to update the data that is found on your database.
2. INSERT: This one is going to insert some new data onto the database you are working with.
3. DELETE: This one is able to delete some of the data that you no longer want on your database.
4. SELECT: This is the same as retrieving some of the data that you would like off that database

Of course, these are just a few of the commands that you are able to do with the SQL language. Anything that you would be able to do with a database to make it work better, to make sure that it has the information inside of it that you need, and that you are able to make the necessary changes to it that you would like can be done with the help of the SQL language in no time at all. With this in mind, we can also work with some of the other commands like Drop and Create to perform some of the other tasks that are needed to really modify the database.

Keep in mind here that each o the relational database systems that you would like to work with will contain one or more objects that will be known as the tables. Like tables that we may have used in our spreadsheets and documents, there will be a name for the table, attributes, rows, and columns.

SQL may seem like it is more of a language that will have a lot of limitations on it, but you will find that many programming professionals are going to find it worth their time to learn more about this. For example, data engineers, data scientists, and data analysis are able to work with SQL in order to help them organize and asses their data, especially when they are working with thousands of points of data. It can be helpful with researchers and marketers as well. This language may be a bit easier to handle than some of the other coding languages that we will bring up, but that does not mean that it won't come with some benefits along the way.

C and C++

C is going to be the first language that we are able to use here and it was developed for Bell Telephone in 1972 by Dennis Ritchie. This one was originally used as a language to help write out the right operating systems since C didn't rely on other programs and didn't have to be rewritten for either hardware or operating systems. C also has an efficient amount of memory management, which is going to allow the programmer to have complete control over when, where, and how to allocate the memory they have.

Programmers like to work with C because it allows them to have the flexibility and control that they want to be compared to some of the other languages. In fact, this was so popular that Ritchie later worked along with Ken Thompson a year after its launch and went to rewrite most of the operating system of UNIX in the C programming language. At the time, operating systems were mostly going to be written in assemble, which works fine, but it is going to produce for us programs that we are only able to run on certain types of CPUs. With this know kind of operating system, you would be able to recompile things, even when using it on different types of computers.

Then in 1979, Bjarne Stroustrup went to develop C++ in Bell Labs as an upgrade or an extension to what we are able to find with the C language. This one also added some new features to the original C language. Now we will find that C++ is often used in embedded types of software, video games, applications that need a lot of memory, audio-video processing, and more.

Many other languages, including C#, Java, and .NET, were going to be derived from the C and the C++ language. Because of this, you will find that you will be able to do a ton of projects, mostly in system software, when you are proficient enough to work with these two languages.

If you are looking into a serious programming career, C is going to be a good language for us to start with, since it is going to follow a few of the more traditional methods of programming that you may want to work with. It is going to seem a bit strange to work with it when you begin but remembers that both o these are going to be languages from the 80s or before, but there are some future updates that will start in 2020 that may make them a bit easier to work with.

Objective C

Another option that we are able to work with is going to be known as Objective C. This one has been around since sometime in the 80s, but it did not gain a lot of popularity right away. It was sold by the original programmers in 1988 to NeXT, which used it for this operating system. Then it was bought up by Apple in 1996 and soon became the main language that was used for programming on the Mac Operating System, along with the iPad, iPod touch, and iPhone.

This is going to be a language that is a superset of C. what this means for us is that this programming language is able to exceed the capabilities of the original counterpart that we have. it is also going to mean that any code that you are able to go through and write out in C can also be used in the Object C programs, without you needing to go through and rewrite or revise any of it.

One thing to take note about here is that you are not able to go backward though. The C programs are going to work find in Objective C, but Objective C programs are not going to work in the C programs that are more traditional. This is mostly because there are a lot of added features that are going to come with Objective C. There are also two specific variants of this language that we are able to take a look at and these include:

1. Objective C++: This is where we are able to work with the C++ code within some of the Object C applications that we have.
2. Objective C 2: This one is going to work similar to the original version of this language, but it is going to add in a few new features, including auto-memory management.

If you are interested in working with some apps that can work on the various Apple products, you may find that mixing the Objective C with Swift on the code, and then using this to create a lot of applications for Apple products is the best way to make all of this happen.

Java

Even though the names sound alike, you will find that Java is not going to be related to JavaScript. Many of the principles of Java were actually built around and then improved upon from the C++ language we talked about before, but you will find that most programmers find the Java language to be more user-friendly overall.

Java is going to be a language that is statically typed, and this allows the programmer to write out the instructions that they want with this in commands of English, rather than relying on numeric codes. It does come with a set of rules, which is the syntax, that you will need to follow. But it is going to be a write once and run anywhere kind of language, which means that both experts and beginners are able to jump onto this language and see some results.

Java has been around since the early 90s. it was a language that was developed for Sun Microsystems by James Gosling and his team and was originally designed to be used on a mobile device of that time. but during the 1996 release, the purpose of this was able to shift to the internet and gave programmers a way to create web pages that were more animated than before.

Today we are going to see that Java is going to be used both offline and online, and it is estimated that 90 percent of the Fortune 500 companies out there are going to use applications that are based on Java to help out with some of their daily operations. Programmers are going to enjoy using this kind of language because it is really secure, it is reliable, it is maintainable, stable, and can be scaled to any kind of project that we want.

You will find that Java is going to be usable in many applications, whether we are talking about desktop apps or mobile apps. It is often going to be the most used in large enterprise applications so you should not be too surprised if a hospital or a bank is going to have an in-house Java developer they want to work with. And if you would like to do any kind of work with computer science, then Java is going to be one of the best options to work with.

Python

To start with, this is a language that was named after the well-known comedy series known as Monty Python. Python is going to be considered one of the easiest to learn coding languages out there for beginners, because it is not going to require all of the parts that some of the other languages do, and you will not need to work with a bunch of fancy 0s and 1s to see it work. It has a nice syntax that is simple and will allow users to write out the commands that they want in English.

There are a lot of companies that are already working with Python today including Yahoo Maps, Dropbox, and YouTube. Along with the other features, the Python language is going to focus on the whitespace, which means that you will not need to spend all of your time writing out thousands of lines of code just to get something going with the code. There are also a lot of libraries of Python that are readily available and that you are able to import and use as a template. And sometimes they are great to get your inspiration from to help you begin your project.

Python is going to be the language of choice for things like machine learning, artificial intelligence, cybersecurity, and data science to name a few. This is why a lot of companies, including Disney and Google, are leading the pack on using these. It is a coding language that can also be used and pretty ideal for scientists who will work on numeric computing projects, or programmers who are focused on some of the video games and web frameworks that are out there.

Python is going to be really easy for us to set up and get to work the way that we want. We just need to download and install the software form the www.python.org website, and we can use it on any of the operating systems that we would like. Once this is installed, you are then able to start off on some of your initial projects.

Many experts are going to recommend the Python language to those who are just getting started with programming and who have never done this kind of work in the past. This is because Python is able to teach us some highly structured methods of writing problems and solutions. However, we have to note that the likesome of the other programming languages, you will find that the learning curve is going to be higher with Python as well. So, if you have already gone through and learned some of another language, you may find that shifting right away to Python is going to bring up a few challenges as well.

If you are choosing a language to code in because of a change in your career, then the Python language is going to be the right one for you. Programmers who know at least a little bit of Python, but especially those who are able to specialize in the Python language will earn the second-highest salary for this in the United States. The only programmers who beat them are those who know how to work with the Ruby language that we will talk about next.

Ruby

This is another language that we are able to spend some time on as well as the Ruby language. This was one that was created in 1995 by Yukihiro Matsumoto. This is a great general-purpose kind of language, which means that it has enough flexibility to do the work that you want from talking to your database to running any of the tools from Google to even creating a few apps that are used online and on websites.

Ruby is going to be associated back to the Rails framework, which is why the phrase "Ruby on Rails" may seem a bit familiar to you. This is because when we are able to combine them, Rails and Ruby can easily transform an idea into a real-world application. A list of the most famous websites that will work with Ruby includes Airbnb, Hulu, Twitter, GitHub, Zendesk, Treehouse, and Urban Dictionary.

Some people may be worried that Ruby is hard to work with because it may not be beginner-friendly as some of the other languages, but this is not true. Not only are you going to find that Ruby has a similar syntax to some of the other popular programming languages, including C+, but we will find that there are many other reasons that Ruby is a flexible coding language to work with including:

1. It has a clean and readable syntax perfect for beginner coders. Commands are going to be pretty self-explanatory.
2. Ruby's functions that are built-in, which beginner developers can use directly into their Ruby scrips.

3. Embeddable into HTML and is linked back to a few other options for databases including DB2, MySQL Sybase, and Oracle.

4. You are able to install it in Windows.

5. Useful for building applications for the internet and intranet.

6. They are highly scalable. This means that you are able to start out small and then change to going big when you are ready.

7. It is going to support a lot of the GUI tools that you would like.

You will find that Ruby is ideal for both beginners and advanced programmers. It is going to be an active community right now of 3500 people just on GitHub and the magic continues to wow coders and companies all of the time. This magic of Ruby is also one of the biggest complaints that a lot of users have. they worry that this language is too powerful that a simple line of code would be able to turn a project into something that is fully functional without the coder really understanding how it turned out this way. this is why you may need to join a community or something else to help you learn more about the coding language and how it works.

C#

This is another language that we are able to learn more about, and it was developed by Anders Hejlsberg and his team to be used Microsoft. C# is a language that used to be known as a clone for Java because of how similar it was of that language when it was released. Today, though, C# is going to be a programming language that is used widely on its own across many applications and industries.

C# is going to be one of the most popularly used languages when it comes o the development of 3D games, but you can use it to help create some dynamic websites as well. C# adopted some of the features of C++ and Java and then stripped them of all of their problematic features, including the macro removal, templates, and multiple inheritances. This made it more modern, easier to work with, cleaner, and a very highly effective language that you are able to work with as well.

C# is a really flexible kind of language, which is why it is going to be a good option as the starting language that you want to use for Windows, games, web applications, and other programs. And since it is going to be derived from some of the other C languages out there, you will find that if you take the time to become more fluent in this language, but you will learn the other languages as fast as possible.

Swift

Swift is a programming language that is loved by Apple developers. It was developed to be used with things like Linux, watchOS, tvOS, iPadOS, macOS, and iOS. And it is a much faster, and cleaner language, compared to some of the other languages that may have been statically typed ahead of it.

Swift is a newer language compared to some of the others because it is used with a lot of the Apple products that customers know and love. It can be taken to work with some of the other types of products as well though, we just need to make sure to watch the functionality to make it work for your needs.

Swift is going to be perfect for those who are going to be the most interested in creating applications for iOS, macOS, watchOS, and tvOS, or use with any Apple products, whether for the Mac or mobile devices. It is also going to be ideal for beginners, not only because Swift reads closely to English, but also since the XCode is going to check out for code for building apps automatically.

Kotlin

The next option that we need to work with is the Kotlin programming language. Kotlin is going to be a programming language that is open-sourced and it is based on the Java Virtual Machine. Kotlin gained widespread attention across the developer community when Google announced back in May 2019 that Kotlin is the preferred language for Android developers.

Kotlin is not going to be designed to be a direct replacement to C++ and Java for Android development but with Google giving the language a blessing as well. You will also find that Android developers might as well go cutting edge knowing that this language will be supported for years to come and has a learning curve too that is easier to work with. Java is an aging language and although it has aged well, Kotlin is still trying to reduce the amount of coding required to get the operations done. Existing developers of Java will find that this transition is smooth and easy since these two work together in many cases.

Rust

And the final language that we are going to take a moment to look over is Rust. This is more of a low-level language that we are able to work on compared to some of the others, but it still has its place on our list. Rust is a newer language on the block and was developed by Mozilla Foundation. It is like a reincarnation of the C++ language, but it is going to have some interesting kinds of improvements compared to some of the other languages.

Like some of the other low-level programming languages, Rust is going to have a low memory footprint, which will make it faster than Java, and that's really what we want to expect since having less English-like statements in the mix will make it easier to translate the machine code that we want.

At the same time, this kind of language is also going to address some of the major weaknesses that are found in C++ and C, such as safety. Basically, Rust is going to come with a lot of safety measures to help ensure that the program is not going to run into any errors when you run the code. Because of the low footprint, you will find that it is easier to consider Rust to develop some of the programs that you want for web applications and embedded devices to name a few. The community that comes with Rust right now is pretty small, but it is a good language to learn and can be easy to work with if you have any experience with the C or the C++ language.

One of the benefits that you are going to see when you are a beginner in the world of programming is that you get to really choose your programming language on any kind of criteria that you would like, such as figuring out how much you enjoy working on one language compared to one of the others. If you start out a project in one language, you can switch over to another one if you find that you really do not like the work that you are doing in it. It is easy for you to try out a few and figure out which one is right for you.

Take a look at some of the different steps that we have discussed in this chapter, and see how this can help you to figure out which of the programming languages are going to be the best for you. Sometimes it depends on what your preferences are, and sometimes it is going to be more important to pick one that you think meets the needs of the project that you would like to work on overall.

Chapter 4: Preparing Yourself for Coding

Now that we have had some time to look through all of the basic terms that come with coding and programming, and we know a bit more about some of the different coding languages that you are able to choose to work with, it is now time for us to work on preparing ourselves to do some of the codings that are going on here. We need to look at how we can get started, how to go about doing some of the practice we need in coding and more. Let's dive into some of the preparation that is needed to help you get your coding done in no time.

Preparing the Vision

The first thing that we need to focus on is how to prepare our vision. This can start when we think about why we really wanted to learn how to code in the first place. For many new programmers, this is because they wanted to be able to make a new program or new software, or something else that does not exist yet. Others may have wanted to do it because they know this can land them that high paying job that they want, and they would like to make sure they are prepared.

There are a lot of motivating factors to learn how to code, so you have to stop and identify what drives you, and then look for the inspiration sources that you will rely on. These are going to encourage you to stay focused on your goals along the way. for a coder, maybe the inspiration would be something like making a new game, working for a big company like Apple, or building a competitor that can go up against Twitter. It could even be something as simple as creating a portfolio of websites.

If it helps, you should consider writing down the vision of what you would like to do. Think about the overall goal that you want to reach, and what this would mean for you overall as well. Preparing your vision is often one of the hardest parts of the whole process, and if you can get it down in writing, and really explore it and get specific, it will help you drive you on, even when some of the coding options get hard.

Getting the Program Structure Prepared

In an earlier chapter, we talked about the importance of working with algorithms and flowcharts when it comes to working with coding. It is not an absolute requirement in many cases, and you may find that it is easy enough to write out a quick piece of software without needing to spend all that much time planning it. But to keep things as efficient as possible, and to make sure that you do not waste as much time having to go back to the drawing board all of the time, it is always a good idea to come up with a solid and secure structure for your program right from the beginning.

Rushing right over to the code editor, without having a good plan in place, is going to be like trying to build up a new house without having a blueprint in hand. The flowcharts and algorithms are going to be useful for helping you to know what will work and what won't, and you will be able to get a feel for your project through them before you even get started. if you don't like the structure or you feel that it lacks some polish, then this is probably true and you need to make some adjustments right from the start.

How to Prepare the Hardware

The really cool thing that you will notice about coding is that you do not necessarily need to have a really fancy computer in order to get it all started. you can even work with a really old Windows XP laptop and get some of the coding done that you want, as long as you make sure that the right software is downloaded and ready to go. Of course, the low-end hardware is going to slow down some of your codings so you may want to find a middle ground with something that is affordable and a little bit newer as well.

This is just to say that coding is not necessarily going to be a huge investment. Your choice in the hardware that you will go with will often depend on where you plan to spend your time coding for the most part. So, let's take a look at these.

If you work in the home and office, you will find that you need to work with a desktop kind of computer. These are going to be the most bang for what you want to do and they are easier to work with as well. The chipsets and mobile components are going to be more expensive and many of the powerful laptops that you may want to use in today's world are going to be thin with a lot of sophisticated engineering. They also come with some of the other components that you are not going to be able to find on desktops.

However, when you are trying to save time and money, the desktop is the best option. These are going to be cheaper to work with, but they do also come with more power and they will not get heated up as much as the others because the performance on them is going to be better. Yes, performance is going to matter when you are trying to compile a program when you want to work with a debugger or an interpreter, or any time that you would like to run a more complicated program.

Picking out the options that you want does not have to be that hard. For the GPU, you want to make sure that there are as many cores as possible. The higher the clock speed that you can get, the better. If you are trying to pick between one with AMD or Intel, just go with the option that is lower in price because they are pretty similar. If you would like to work with Windows 10, then working with 8 GB of RAM will be the best, but higher is even better. More RAM just means that your system is less likely to get bogged down when you are trying to run a lot of applications and parts at the same time.

A good display setting on the monitor is also going to be important to some of the coding that you want to use. You want to be able to see the codes that you are trying to write out at the time, rather than trying to guess whether you were able to get it to work or not. The higher the resolution that we are able to get on the screen, the better for everyone.

Sometimes though, you will do some of the codings that need to be done from the road, rather than from your home or your office. This may mean that you need to pick out a laptop in order to get the work done. Picking a laptop that is geared more towards coding is going to add in some complications because all of the laptops are going to bring you some kind of compromise. You will really need to focus down to your preferences and what strengths you think you need in your own laptop that will help you to make a decision.

Of course, the first issue that you want to address is the portability. This is one o the main reasons why you wanted to work a laptop in the first place. A heavier laptop is going to be higher quality and last longer, but a lighter laptop is going to make it more travel-friendly in the long run. You have to spend some time picking out the best balance between the two of them for your needs.

If you are already working with a powerful desktop to help with this, and you just plan to do a bit of traveling and only need to code on it sometimes, then working with a thin or a light laptop is probably just fine. You may have to sacrifice a bit on the power in the CPU and the typing experience, but the portability and battery life can be nice. You can also work with the cloud storage devices in order to help you to access the information that you need out of that laptop and more to make things easier, even when you are traveling.

If you are not working with a desktop and your laptop is older, it may be time for you to work with a little more advanced kind of laptop to get things done overall. You may find that going with one that has a 45-watt TDP processor is going to be a good option, and keep in mind that Intel is going to be the company that dominates in this.

Preparing the Software

Going along with some of the goals of the rest of this guidebook and keeping your costs for working in programming down as much as possible, we are going to take a look a some of the free or low cost options that you are able to work with no matter what coding language you want to work with. There is going to be a lot of free information that you can use, and you will find that even some of the free tools that you are able to use have become really powerful as well.

There are a lot of options that you are able to use when it comes to working with these types of software. For example, we could work with flowcharting software. If you would like to draw out a flowchart, having some software that can take what you are working with and clean up the chart and make it as organized as possible can be important. You can choose to work with your own software and add it to your computer, but the http://www.draw.io is a good option to use if you would like to just draw the flowchart out and you don't need to use the software for it.

Another option that we are able to focus on is some of the web development tools that are out there. C++ is going to be a good programming language that you are able to work with when it is time to learn a few of the basics of coding, but you want to be hands-on as much as possible. You can work with a good sandbox to handle some of this. If you want to work with the HTML language, for example, you can work with https://htmlcodeeditor.com. The user interface is not going to be all that elegant compared to some of the other options, but it is going to provide us with a live preview that makes it easier to play around with the codes that we have and can help us to see what it will result in when things are done. You will not have to wait for things to compile, though you will be restricted to just some of the code in HTML.

There are other versions that you are able to work with if you choose to search them out when you are coding. It is all going to depend on what you would like to see with some of the work that you see, and what you would like to be able to get done. But there are many web development tools that will allow you to try out your codes and see how they are going to behave when everything is said and done in the process.

The next thing that we will need to focus on is the source code editors. Whether you plan to do the more nomadic route and work with some pure raw coding, or you want to work with an IDE that has all of the features that you are looking for, it is always a good idea to come in with one, and sometimes more, code editors that you are able to rely on as well. Some of these editors are not going to be heavy apps to work with, which means that you are able to go through using the free version and seeing the same results that you want.

You may also want to consider some of the bells and whistles when it comes to your code editor. For example, if you would like to have some support for debugging, then you would find that working with something like Microsoft Visual Studio would be able to provide you with this when you are working with the source code editors.

The next thing on the list that we need to focus on here is the IDE. When we are ready to move past what we are able to do online with a language like HTML, you may find that many of the languages are going to require you to have an IDE so that you are able to get all of the work done. These are just the environments that you use in order to write out some of the codes that you need in many languages like Python.

There are often free IDE's that are available in the files when you download a language to your computer. This helps to keep the costs down, and often they have plenty of the features that you are looking for so you won't have to go out and get a different one. However, if there are some specific features that you would like to have in one of the IDE"s that you are doing, then this is something to consider along the way as well. If you are going to download another IDE to use, take a look at whether it will provide the features that you want if it is going to work with the language that you want, and how much it is going to cost for you to use them.

Another option that can be helpful when you are working with the coding language of your choice is the browser extensions that you would like to have. no matter which language you are planning on working with, you will find that having an extension that allows you to do some work online can be useful. There are some languages that may work better than the others, but this does not mean that you are not able to use the option that you want to work on websites and other databases that may be online as well.

There are many browser extensions that you are able to use, we just need to make sure that we know how to do the proper coding, and that we make sure that the extension that we are trying to work with is set up to work with whatever coding language we are trying to use on that website as well.

These are just the start of what you are able to do with some of the freeware that is out there for you to work with. Coding can get really tiring to work with, especially if you are not seeing a lot of ends when it comes to the project you have. it is possible for a coder to get something that is known as coder's block, and it is a situation that is going to be really similar to what we will see with the writer's block.

One way to help prevent this kind of block coming up and ruining the experience that you have with coding is to find some fun ways to stay motivated. And one tool that you are able to use to make both of these things happen is known as Habitica. This is going to take more of a gamification approach when it comes to the coding process and will help you to feel like some of the coding that you are working on is going to be more of a game rather than work.

Another issue that it seems a lot of programmers are going o deal with is handling different platforms with the same language. Linux is still one of the best platforms to use when it is time to handle your coding, but restarting your computer and then getting the Linux system to show up on your computer is going to make the transition not that much fun and your machine may not be able to handle this. There are options, like the VMWare Player where you will be able to get the Linux system to show up on one part of your screen, while still keeping the Windows up as well.

This can be useful for some of the coders who want to work with the Windows system, or at least want to make sure that their code is going to work on both of the systems along the way. It is something to at least take a look at and see if it is going to be able to do what you would like.

It is also possible that you are going to do some work with coding and math, and you could run into a few problems along the way. When you do encounter some of these problems, you can work with a calculator that is known as SpeedCrunch. This is not going to be like some of the other calculators that you will use because it is going to provide us a text box that has a command line where you are able to type in the equations of math that you would like to be able to use.

If you are like a lot of the programmers out there who are working on a really big coding project to help handle some of the issues that are going to show up on your program, you may find that working with something like a flowchart of your program is not going to be quite the right thing that you want to work with. You have to come up with some kind of method to use that will track the status of the project, especially when there is more than one person working on that same project.

The good news is that there are a lot of project management tools that you are able to work with along the way that will make sure that you are able to keep the vision and the focus on the project, even when there are many people working on the same project, at different times, throughout the development of the project. You can even find that some of these are going to provide us with the roadmap that we need to see what is happening and will allow everyone to get on the same page about the whole thing as they go.

As we can see, there are a lot of different parts that are going to come together when we are working with the beginning of our own coding language as well. We need to make sure that we have all of the necessary parts set up and ready to go without having to worry about a big delay in what is going to happen with some of the work that we are getting done as well. Make sure to take a look at some of the different options that are available within the topics that we discussed in this guidebook, and then you will be set to work on some of your own codes, no matter which language you decide to go with.

Chapter 5: Code Resources to Help You Get Started

Even though we have been able to take some time to look at a lot of the different parts that are going to come with the coding that we want to get done, it is time for us to spend a little more time here checking out some of the other resources that are available for the codes that we want to write. Even if you think that you already know a ton about coding and what will come with it, you should find that there is nothing out there that will stop you from looking at more of the resources that are present with this, and help you to expand the knowledge that you already have.

Programming languages are going to be beasts that change all of the time, and some of the IDE's and frameworks that you will have to work with will get better, and more complicated, over time as well. New, cutting-edge kinds of features are going to be added. So if you would like to keep up with the changes and maybe even go after a programming career in the future, it is important that you are able to keep up with these changes. Let's take a look at some of the different resources that you are able to consider when it is time to work with coding, no matter what language you are going to work with.

Interactive Sites

In the past few chapters, we have taken some time to look at a few of the interactive websites that are out there, the ones that are going to allow you to test some of the codes that you want, and then run them online to see how they are going to work for some of your own needs. As a beginner, these are some of the best websites that you can work with because the compiling work is going to be done on the servers of that computer so you will not need to work with a powerful PC in order to see how some of your own codings is going to work. You just can use these sites as a good way to practice some of the codings that you would like to get done.

For example, if you are working with C++ and HTML< you will find have some of their own options as well. But if you would like to take a look at how to work with a wide variety of the coding languages out there, then you would want to visit the site https://paizo.io. This one is going to offer the support and more that you need dozens of other languages. It is going to help us to work with some of the languages that we have already spent time talking about in this guidebook including Swift, Objective C, Python, PHP, C# and Bash. You only need to set up an account and you will be able to go through and use this for your needs in coding.

If you still find that you are running out of ideas on what you would like to be able to do with some of your codes, but you still want a way to flex out your skills in coding, another option to check out is going to be coderbyte.com. This is going to come up with a new approach to helping you get better with some of the codings that you want to do. It is going to offer us a series of courses, in the form of a video, that you can watch to learn the basics of other languages that are there. there are also some sections that are going to handle some of the algorithms that you want to be able to get done as well.

The thing that is the most exciting when you are working with this website is that it is going to provide us with a lot of problems that we are able to work on and solve so that we can learn with more experience. You can really challenge yourself when you do it on your own, or you get the option to work with others who do this kind of thing and see how they would work with that situation or that challenge as well.

This is just a really interactive method that you are able to use when it is time to handle some of the codings that you want to get done. It allows people who learn in a variety of manners to figure out which method is going to be the best one to help them out. Whether you like to learn on your own, get help from others, or even learn in a more interactive manner from watching a video, then this is an option that you are able to do with this website.

The Discussion Boards

Another option that we are able to go with other than some of the interactive boards that we just talked about, is to take a look at how we are able to look through some of the many discussion boards that are out there. These boards are going to be really popular in any language that you can find when it comes to exchanging ideas in coding to asking for help from beginners.

A lot of people right now want to be able to learn how to code, whether we are talking about students or those who are looking to make a big change in their careers. Get yourself into one or two of these communities, at a minimum because you are going to be able to learn a lot of information there, and that is going to make life so much easier when you get started. And when you are on one of these boards, never be scared to ask the questions that you have, this is how you will learn.

To start with, StackOverflow is going to be one of the biggest public Q&A websites that has more than 17 million program-related questions that are already posted. You can even find jobs that relate to programming here and gain some reputation points when you help out some of the other people who are looking for answers as well. You can lurk around here on your own and you only need to create a new account when you would like to leave a comment or a question.

This site and others are going to have coders present who come from all parts of the world. This means that you will be able to ask all of the questions that you want about programming in that language you want to learn, and someone is likely to come in and have an answer for you.

Programming is even going to have its own social media presence that you should know about as well. As long as you are comfortable with bringing on that real name of yours, rather than a fake or hidden name, to help you to join in on the discussion bards and more, you will be able to join this presence. Of course, we will be able to find this on Facebook, but there are other options as well where you are able to ask questions, share information, and learn along the way.

It would be impossible for us to go through and end this section without taking a look at the popular site of Reddit. For those who have not been able to work with Reddit, this is going to be a website for large discussions where people are able to come in and create some of their own boards and post topics and links that will help them to get some of their work done.

Sometimes this site is going to make it a bit trickier to reach out to the communities that you want with programming because there are a lot of user-generated kind of content out there, but you will find that when you get to one of those groups, it is going to be the best way for you to learn a lot of the different types of coding and the functions and more that you would want to spend your time on here.

It is also worth noting here that a lot of the higher-level programming languages have been around for a much longer time frame compared to some of the other social media and more that we will use. Before these kinds of sites existed, people would interact on forums, and there were many of these around for you to use. Consider taking a look at some of these if you still need help with some of the codings you are doing.

Video Resources

Out of the billions of videos that are found on YouTube, a good amount of them are going to be related back to programming in some manner. It is not going to be the most obvious choice that you will make here since it is hard to directly show the source code on there. but there are many YouTubers out there who are able to explain some of the codings and show you the tips and tricks that you need to get it all done. And because these individuals can now make money through YouTube, it is likely that more of them are going to be coming out before too long.

If you find that you are stuck on one of the coding topics that you want to work with, then it is a good idea to take a look at some of the different video resources that you are able to find, including on YouTube and other places as well. You can search for the language that you want to learn from, and even from some of the specific codes that you would like to get help with and find some of the information that would make it easier to get this language complete.

The Games

Learning how to get through some of the codings that you want so you can create some of your own programs may not seem like that much fun and you may feel like there isn't going to be any kind of reward in the end. Then if you hit some roadblocks along the way, you will find that it is going to make it even harder for you to get some of the results that you would like. This is why many professional programmers are going to suggest that you take a break when things get tough, and maybe consider doing a little bit of gaming. We are not meaning just some random gaming though. We are going to work with some that can help you to learn how to code better and can even increase the amount of productivity that you will enjoy.

We are able to start out simple here, with a typing game. You will have your mechanical keyboard there, but if you feel that the typing you are doing is still a little sluggish compared to where you would like to find it, then there is a game that is known as TypeRacer that you are able to work with. You can go online and find a bunch of free online typing games that will provide you with some confidence as well as a small boost in the confidence that you have to code faster.

Now, we need to move on to a real coding game, rather than one that just works on how fast you are able to type out your codes. A good place to start is going to be with CodeCombat. This is a good game to work with if you want to handle the CoffeeScript, Python, or JavaScript languages for your needs. You will be able to play the game, even if you do not have any experience with these kinds of coding languages because it is going to have more of a hand-holding kind of approach to teaching you how to make things work. You will get a lot of experience in this and some of the help that you need along the way.

If you are still uncertain about which of the many programming languages you would like to learn along the way, you can still find a few games out there that are going to help you to at least learn some of the basics that come with coding and will put some of the concepts in front of you, including the conditional statements and the variables.

You would probably find that working with something like the Minecraft Code can be a lot of fun. Yes, this is a game that can teach you a lot of coding and is going to be one of the biggest players when it comes to getting people to code along the way. in fact, it has made coding as simple as possible so that anyone is able to come in and give it a try. There are many different coding games that are based on this so that you are able to get the practice that you need.

If you are not that fond of the Minecraft idea, although you should take a look at it because of the educational factor, and not get hung up on the fact that it is kind of a kid game, there are still a few other options that you are able to choose when you want to learn how to work with coding. Depending on the game, you may or may not need to know some of the basics when it comes to the programming language that you want to learn, such as Python or Java, but you can catch on to some of those basics quickly and move on from there.

The Hardware

If you would like to get some of your children to get more involved with coding, you may find that working with a book and other references may have a lot of good information, but it probably will not get you far with them being interested in what you are showing them however, there are some people who have a passion for what is known as STEM learning who have come up with some hardware that can make the hardware that is needed for coding to be more relatable and accessible.

A good place to start is with the Piper Computer Kit. This is going to be a small computer that is less than $300 and will have a screen and a lot of other puzzles that will help children to think their way through one of the challenges when applying some of the basic logic that comes with coding. It is going to be a great way for kids to learn more about coding and to really see it in the positive light than they should.

For adults, extra hardware is not something that they really need to learn or use from in order to get better with coding, apart from some of the things that we talked about in an earlier chapter here. But if you would like to find a new way to learn some of the codings that you want, and maybe you are not feeling the other methods, you may find that working with the Raspberry Pi devices is the right option for you to work with.

The hardware that comes with this is going to be all for the person who wants to use programming as a hobby as this is going to be the size of a tiny motherboard that is about the size of a credit card. You can start simply by buying a nice case for the board if you would like and this turns it into a small computer that you are able to use to code online and more. There are a ton of different options that you are able to do with this and a simple search online will show you how great this will be.

While the point of this guidebook is not to spend our time talking about the Raspberry Pi devices and all that they can do, even though they are pretty marvelous with all of the options, you will find that this is a good example of some of the things that you are going to be able to do when it comes to working with coding and learning how to make it happen. This is just one of the methods though and you will quickly see that with a bit of imagination and exploring around, you will soon be able to do some of the codings that you would like, without all of the issues along the way.

Take some time here to make sure that you are set up and ready to go. Each programmer is going to be a bit different in what they would like to work with, which programming language is the right for them, and so much more. What works well for one coder is not always going to work the best for another coder along the way. but all of these resources can be useful and will ensure that you are able to see the benefits that you want, and actually learn how to code in no time at all.

Chapter 6: Tips and Tricks to Make Your Coding Successful

Now it is time to get on to one of the fun parts of this guidebook. Whether you are someone who is just getting started with coding, you are a budding programmer, or you have been working with this as a developer for some time, you wills till find that coding can be a journey that is never really over. And you need to make it your goal to never settle with the skills that you just learned or the ones that you always have.

What we mean here is that we need to always approach the coding that we want to do with a more forward-thinking mindset and then figure out ways that we are able to improve ourselves over time until we make the programs that we would like. There are millions of people who are so into coding and love to do it, but that doesn't mean that learning a new language is not going to be a bit of a challenge over time as well. Taking some baby steps, and working with some of the tips and tricks that we are going to discuss in this guidebook can help you to become a better coder, and will improve your productivity and reduce the amount of frustration that you have.

Have a Backup System You Can Trust

The first thing that we need to discuss in this chapter is the backup system. We have now reached the point in this guidebook where there is not going to be a good excuse for losing any of your data. This is because we have a lot of great technology that can help us out with this. For example, we are going to work with something known as cloud computing in many cases that is able to integrate with an operating system so that it only takes a few quick steps before we are able to make sure our source code is backed up and ready to go.

Sure, there are going to be some decompilers that you are able to work with that are able to transform a compiled program back into the source code if you would like, but it is going to be a lot better for everyone if you are able to store the source code in a place like OneDrive or another similar kind of service that is out there. you will find that most source code files are going to be small, and when you use some of the apps that are out there, like WinRAR, you are able to make these files even smaller through compression.

It is always really important to back up some of your files, and places like Windows 10 is going to make this as simple as possible. When you are working with Windows, you would be able to create a folder in the OneDrive folder and put all of the projects and source codes there. Open up that folder and then observe the status of the backup. If there is a green checkmark that will show up next to the code, then you know that the code is already going to be backed up on your cloud.

If you go through and look at this and do not see the green checkmark, then you need to take on a few more steps in order to make this work. For example, you may have to launch the OneDrive app from the Start menu and then sign onto the account that you have with Microsoft. Once you are done doing the backup, you will be able to copy these files over to a flash drive or even a hard drive that disconnects from your computer just in case there is something going on with your account or even with OneDrive when you need it most.

You need to make sure that you are not necessarily putting all of your eggs into one single cloud basket either. Many programmers like to rely on more than one of these cloud services at a time to make it easier and safer for some of the codes that they are using. A good option to work with is the Dropbox option. It is similar to what we are going to see with OneDrive, and you can easily go through and have both of these apps running in the background to give you all of the storage space online that you are looking for.

Then once you have had some time to get better at programming and find that you are more of a professional with this, you could consider uploading your codes to other places like GitHub. ON top of this, the cloud services will make it convenient in order to share the source code that you have with others.

Sort out the Workspace with Some Virtual Desktops

Another thing that we need to take a look at is how you are able to sort out the space that you are working in to help you get the best results. We already mentioned a bit before how these dual monitors are going to help us to improve some of the productivity that we are going to see when it comes to working in coding. However, not all programmers are going to be able to handle this or make this work.

For these people, you may find that working with a second monitor is going to be one of the best investments to make this happen. You have to spend the extra money and may need to make sure that your desk is going to have some of the extra space to get it all set up. Maybe you would prefer to do it on a laptop instead as well. But you will find that both Mac and Windows 10 are going to come with features that will let you sort some of your open apps and windows in one or more desktops if you would like.

If you are doing this in Windows 10, it is going to be known as the Virtual Desktop. But if you are doing it on Mac, it is going to be known as Spaces. The first desktop that you are using is going to be the code editor or the IDE on the full screen, and then the other one that you are working with could be the flowchart that you are working with. It is all about how you want to make this work, and what seems to make the most sense for you.

The best thing that is going to show up with some of this virtual desktop is the ease of being able to change up the desktop that you would like to work with. A three or four hand sliding gestures on the touchpad is going to quickly take us from one desktop over to the next. With a mouse setup and a keyboard, you are able to hold Windows and then hit the Tab to make sure that you can get the timeline and create a new desktop virtually. And it is as simple as Ctrl + Windows + Left or Right to help you get through the different desktops that you have.

Print Off the Cheat Sheets

Another thing that we are able to work with is some of the cheat sheets that are going to help us to get some of the work done that we need. While the Internet is going to provide us with a ton of programming guides on all of the different languages, we still need to spend some time Googling our way to them and then sift through the references in order to find out the information that we need. If you want to know the syntax of a command or some of the clever methods that you can use to write the statement, you have to go through this process to get it done.

You may find that many of the IDE's that you want to work with along the way is going to come with some auto-complete functions to make some of the coding easier. But the beginner-friendly source code editors will often lack this neat feature. And a good way to deal with this and to make sure that you are able to find what you would like in the process, without having to worry about doing all of the searchings is to print off some cheat sheets to make it work

Now, you will find that there are two main ways that you are able to do this, and the first method is going to be a simple one to work with. When we are talking about the first one, we need to work with a Google search and then look for a few cheat sheets for the programming language that we want to do online. Then we can click on our Images tab and see some of the print-friendly sheets. The higher the resolution that you are able to get the document printed off, the easier it is going to be to get things done.

Then you are able to take this kind of cheat sheet and pint it up somewhere that you will be able to see. This provides us with an immediate reference to the syntax and to some of the other important information that you will need on that programming language, without wasting time or worrying about the space it is going to take up on your computer.

There is a second method that we are able to work with as well. This second method is that we want to go through and design one of our own cheat sheets that include the information that is the most important for us. This is going to require us to do some research ahead of time, but it does allow you the benefit of controlling your content, the design, and the layout that you want to work with. If your printer is not able to go through and print off some of the big pages that you need, you may want to consider making more than one kind of cheat sheet and then taping it together to get the best results. You will find that this is often one of the best and the low-cost option, that you can use rather than working with a second monitor.

Mess Around with the Interface of the Code Editor

The next thing that we need to take a look at is the interface of the code editor, and mess around with it a bit in order to figure out what is going to work, what we like, and what will work the best for the kinds of codes that we want to use. IDEs and source code editors are going to be customizable, and this is for a good reason. The reason for this is that it caters to as many different programmers as possible. Even the very basic of these editors, like the Notepad from Windows, is going to allow you a chance to change things like the size of the font and the type of the font.

The neat thing that you are going to be able to see with some of the major operating systems like Windows and Mac operating system is that you are able to download the fonts that you want from the Web and then apply them to any of the apps that you would like in order to help support the customization of the interface. There happens to be a lot of great fonts out there that are friendly to code, and you just need to go out and search for them.

You can choose the right kind of font that you want to use based on what seems to be the easiest on your own eyes, and what will get you more in the mood to work on some of these longer projects that you have. do not forget that you are also able to make some adjustments that are needed to the size of the font as well because it is going to help us to spot the syntax errors and bugs that are in there as well.

This isn't the stopping point either. There are some other parts of the interface that you are able to customize as well. Some of the code editors out there that you may want to work with are going to have some themes that you want to work with. For example, you are able to work with a dark theme, which is going to be a good one for some programmers because they will find it reduces distractions. You can also go through and look for the mode of Full Screen in order to hide things like the taskbar. This helps you to stay on your coding, rather than being tempted to work with your social media feeds or something else when you really have your momentum.

Try Out Some Music

Coding is going to require us to have a lot of concentration to get things done. This is because you are going to be responsible for handling a lot of problems all at once. Are there some potential flaws that are going to be found in your algorithm? Are you wording the statement that you want to use in the proper manner? Is the formulates for math correct, are there too many variables, is the program secure, or should you go through and reduce how many conditional statements you are working with?

These kinds of questions are going to end up leading to a lot of stress, especially if you find that you are not moving towards the answer that you are hoping for in the process. When you have some of these periods that are causing you some anxiety, you will find that music is going to be a differentiator. If you do run into some issues with the coding that you are doing, then you should just turn on some music from any source that you would like, and then see if this is what you need in order to solve your problems and see if this is going to be able to make things easier.

Sometimes you just need to get out of your own head. If you sit there in the silence, you are more likely to let the mind wander and it is not going to work on the things that you would like. If you let these worries get to you, then you need to make sure that you cut that out, and music, or some other background noise, will make it easier for you to get the results that you want with some of your codings.

Remember that Smartphone

One thing that we need to remember when we are doing some work here is that we are able to put our smartphone to some good use in the process. You can find that these smartphones, even if they seem pretty simple, are going to be a great tool that you are able to use to make coding just a little bit easier for your needs.

Just look at some of the options that are out there like the iOS App Store and the Google Play Store. And it will not take you too long to find that there are a ton of mobile tools that you are able to use to assist with your coding. Some of the apps such as the ones by developer SoloLearn come in the form of a course that you can actually take in order to learn a new language.

So, if you find that you really do need to take a break from the keyboard and all of the work that you are doing, and it seems like it is just too much for you to handle for a bit, then it may be time to work with some of the great apps that are on your smartphone. You can set aside a bit of time each day to learn how to use a coding language that you right, and do all of this from your own phone. Don't forget that your phone can also come with the Kindle app and that you are able to get the guides and the codes and more that you need, right in your smartphone along the way.

Ask for Help When Needed

There are times when you will need some help with the work that you do. It would be nice if we were able to figure out all of the work that we need to get done on coding on our own, but this is just not the way that things are going to work, especially as a beginner. And there is nothing wrong with asking others for help when we need it, we just need to make sure that we are doing it in the right manner.

First, we have to make sure that we are as organized on this process as possible. You do not want to waste the time of the person who is coming in and helping you out. if you are not organized and ready to explain what is wrong with the code, and what you have tried in the past already (and you should have done at least a little bit of troubleshooting ahead of time), then you are not ready to ask someone else for help. If someone is being kind enough to be there and help you out with a problem that you have, then you need to be kind enough to not waste their time.

There are a few things that you can organize and write down before you talk to the person who will help you out. Start by listing out what you want the program to do. This will help the coder to know what you are trying to do, so they can ix it in the manner that you would like. This is simple enough, you can just provide a quick summary of what you would like to see done in some of the code that you are doing, and then work from there.

The next thing that you need to discuss is where the problem is happening. You can explain why the program is not working, or at least where you first started to see some problems. Describing the problem is often going to really help the other person and the description may be enough that they will be able to tell you right away what is going on and how you can fix it.

And while we are here, we need to make sure that we tell the other person what we have tried out already to get this problem fixed. It is never a good idea to go into this without trying something. It will frustrate the other person to hear that you are not even trying to fix your own issues, and you will not become a better coder if you are not able to fix some of these issues on your own as well. You need to try out at least a few troubleshooting options before asking for help, and then explain these to the person who is coming in to help you.

This helps to show that you have at least given it a good try and are not just relying on someone else to do all of the work for you. And it ensures that the other person is not retrying things that you already did, effectively saving them time and allowing them to get to the root of the problem faster than ever before. Make sure to try out a few things, and then list them out so that the other person can see what you have tried to accomplish.

Code with a Friend

Coding alone can be boring. And you will no learn as much along the way. the best way to improve some of your own coding skills and to learn as much as possible from coding along the way is to find a friend who wants to learn the language and see if they will do it along with you. This is sometimes hard to do, especially when it comes to finding someone who is willing and wanting to learn the same coding language as you do. But even if you are able to find someone who is able to work with you online or somewhere else, this can make a difference in the success that you will see with coding.

Coding with a friend is a good way to stay motivated. Both of you can share ideas, and encourage each other to keep on coding along the way. When times get tough with the coding world you are able to work with this person and both of you stay on track. Plus, when you are working with someone else to complete a project, it is going to seem like less work in the first place.

Coding with a friend can also be more fun. You get to work along with someone, rather than feeling like you are closed up in a room without anyone else to talk to all of the time. When you take breaks you have someone there to take them with you. When you need a good laugh to break up the tension when the code is not doing what you would like, you will have a friend there to do it with you. It just makes coding a bit better.

But one of the best benefits of doing all of this with a friend is that you can bounce ideas off of them, and they off of you, and share what might work to solve a particularly tough problem along the way. if you have ever been stuck with some of the work that you are doing, and you find that it seems a lot easier when you have someone else to talk it out with and discuss what changes need to be made at that time.

Only Do a Bit of Coding At a Time

As a new programmer, you are most likely really excited to jump in and try out some of the things in coding that we have already spent quite a bit of time working on here. That is great news, but you also have to consider whether this is a smart idea to just jump in and spend hours on coding at a time, especially as a beginner. It is motivating to have all of that energy and want to get started as quickly as possible on some of the work that you are doing, but you do want to make sure that you are not going crazy with the work, and not taking a break at all.

There are a few issues that are going to come up with this one. First, it is going to wear you out of coding pretty quickly if you do it in this matter. You will find that if you spend hours on coding all of the time, or at least in the first few days, it is going to leave you feeling tired and drained in the process. You will have trouble concentrating on what is going on and will start to find it a bit boring. Even with something that you love and are good with, you will find that spending hours on it without breaks and without figuring out how to make it more fun can really ruin the experience.

Taking lots of breaks, and making sure that the work that you are doing is broken up into smaller pieces is one of the best ways to ensure that you are going to be able to get your program to work the way that you would like. Maybe as a beginner split it up into a few fifteen-minute sessions, with some breaks to grab a drink or walk around to clear your head. You can add on some longer times if you would like later on, once you are more comfortable with what you are doing in coding. But in the beginning, we need to make sure that we keep it short and sweet and see how much easier that will make the coding overall.

Another issue is what happens with all of the errors and how frustrating that can be. If you spend two hours writing out a lot of code, and you forget to run it or check on it regularly, this is going to make a big mess. It is unlikely that you are able to get started with some of the codings without having errors, and the longer you go without checking the code that you are doing, the harder it is going to be overall.

If you didn't test any of the code that you were doing along the way, the whole thing is going to turn into a big mess now. You will end up with no idea what to do with some of the programs that you have, you will have to search through all of that code, which could be pages and pages long, and you are going to get sick of coding pretty quickly.

A better option that you are able to work with here is the idea of doing a little bit of coding at a time, rather than the long spurts. If you are able to test every few minutes along the way to see how the program is doing, that is even better. You will find that doing this allows us a chance to really figure out where the errors are because you better know where the error stared in the first place, and where you should look for it.

So basically, make things as easy for yourself as you can when it comes to programming, and take breaks, know when it is time to stop because you are getting frustrated, and test the codes that you are doing on a regular basis to see if there are errors and other things that you need to fix. Doing this is going to make it a lot easier to work with and can ensure that you will be able to handle the coding, even as someone who is just getting started.

Look at Some of the Available Libraries

Sometimes the best way to determine which coding language you would like to go with is going to be as simple as looking at some of the features that they offer, and how these are going to help you get some of the codings that you want to be done in no time at all. For example, if you want to work with machine learning, you would heavily consider the Python language because it has a ton of libraries that work well with machine learning, deep learning, artificial intelligence, and so much more in the process.

Each of the languages that you want to work with will be able to provide us with some good libraries that we are able to consider depending on what we would like to see with some of the codings. You can take a look online to see what is going to be the best option for what you would like to accomplish in the coding that you do.

Depending on the libraries that you would like to use, you may find that some of them are going to be open-sourced and free for you to use. Many coders like to stay with these because it allows them to do some of the codings that they need, without having to be worried about the added costs. There are some of these libraries though that is going to cost a little bit more and are not going to be free to work with. These usually come to some third-party that will add in some new features and more. You have to judge whether these are the right ones for you to use or not.

Consider How You Will Use the Code in the Future

Sometimes the best way to consider which coding language you would like to work with is to consider how you would like to use the code, or what kind of application you are hoping to make in the process as well. This is going to ensure that you are really able to make the code work the way that you want, and will make it so much easier for us to see some results in the process as well.

Each of the coding languages that we are going to take a look at will have different types of options that we are able to work with as well. For example, if you would like to do some work online, then working with HTML, CSS< or JavaScript is going to be the best. The C, C#, and C++ languages are all good for some of the higher-level programs that you want to work with, such as creating your own games. And then the Python language is a good general-purpose language that can handle a lot of different things at a time and can be helpful with some of the more complicated tasks that you want to do, including machine learning and more.

While many of these languages can be used for more than one type of program or application, many times they are going to have something that makes them special, something that is going to make it really easy for them to get things done. And learning which one is going to be a specialist in some of the coding that you would like to do is going to make a big difference in the amount of success that you will see, and how much motivation you will get when it comes to working with any kind of coding language.

There is nothing wrong with you going through and learning more than one language if you would like. This should not be done at the same time because that is going to really cause some confusion and may make you mix up some of the syntax work that you are doing along the way. But another thing to note here is that once you have been able to get the basics of one language down, it is going to be a lot easier for you to catch some of the basics of another language. They share a lot of information and more with one another, and learning one can make others easier.

There are a lot of things that you are able to do when it comes to learning how to code. And it is likely that you will be able to find a good coding language to work with, no matter what your goals are, which one you see as the easiest to work with, and what kind of application you would like to work with overall. But the tips that you are able to focus on here will be similar, no matter which kind of coding language you would like to go with. When you are ready to learn a bit more about how to get the most out of coding as a beginner, and you want to make sure that you are set up and can do well with your coding, make sure to check out this guidebook to get started.

Chapter 7: How to Pick Out Our Coding Language

The next thing that we are going to spend some time on in this guidebook is a look at how to pick out the right coding language for your needs. You have to make sure that you are starting off with the right coding language for your needs. This can be based on your own personal preferences along the way, which one seems to fit with you, which one is going to serve you the most in your career goals if you are working with some of these to help you with that, which one works with data science, and even which one is going to help you to get your project done in no time at all.

There are so many things that you are able to focus on when it comes to working with a coding language, and you have to take some careful consideration before you choose any of the different coding languages that are out there. There are so many good ones that you are able to focus on, that spending time with one that is not right for your own needs doesn't make all that much sense at all. With this in mind, we need to consider some of the following to help us go with the right coding and programming language for our own needs.

What Kind of Projects Will You Do?

One of the first things that we need to consider when it comes to working on a language and trying to pick out which language we would like to work with, is what kinds of projects we would like to work within the beginning. Some coding languages are going to need to work the best when it comes to one project over another. For example, you may want to consider working with HTML or JavaScript if you are working with a project that has to do with websites or online, and C+ for a higher-level project or game that you have in mind.

You have to really understand the project that you want to work with and then work from there. the more that you know about the parts of your code, and what you want them to do, the easier it is to figure out which of the many great coding languages out there are going to be able to help you to get this done.

So before you go through with this, you will need to consider what you would like to accomplish with the language when you are all done with learning some of the basics. You should have this in mind from the beginning so you make sure you use the right language. What features do you want in the application, what kind of process do you want to use, and more. This should help to lead us a little bit in the right direction when it comes to what kind of coding language that you would like to work with.

Do You Want to Work with Data Science?

One reason that a lot of programmers and even beginners would like to work with any kind of programming language is that it is going to help them out with some projects like machine learning, artificial intelligence, and data science. These are all important options that you are able to add into your business, and will help you to really see some results with how you meet with your customers, provide them with some of the products and services that they want, to solve some of the most important questions that your business has, and even will ensure that you are going to beat out the competition, no matter what kind of industry you are in.

All companies, no matter their industry, are able to benefit when they decide to spend some time on data science. To keep it simple, data science is where we will gather up a lot of data, sort it out and organize it into a database, and then put it through an algorithm that can reveal a lot of insights and patterns in the data so we can use them for our own needs.

Going through the data on our own is going to be impossible, and it is going to really make it hard for us to do in a manual manner. But when we push it through some of the right algorithms we can learn the information and see what is found inside of it is going to be fast, efficient, and more. And the thing that will run these algorithms, and will ensure that we get the accurate results that we need, are some of these coding languages.

If you would like to work with data science in your business, then coding languages are going to be important. These algorithms are the heart of data science. While there are a lot of other parts that come with a good data science project, we can't get through the data and see the right insights and predictions that we need without working on these algorithms ahead of time. And we have to make sure that we know some coding and have the right libraries and extensions to go with these languages, to make it work.

The most common language to help handle some of this data science projects that you want to do is Python. This one is simple, easy to learn, and will really have some of the power that we need in order to help us to see some of the results that we want. Plus, it is going to have a lot of libraries and extensions that we want to work with that can help with data science, machine learning, and deep learning. There are some other languages that can help you out with this as well. It all depends on what you would like to handle when it comes to this kind of project.

If you are not planning on working with Python for this, then we need to go through and figure out which one is going to be the best for some of our needs as well. You can do some of the research that you need to figure out which extras and libraries, and which languages are going to be the best for your needs along the way.

Which One Speaks to You?

If you read through the third chapter in this guidebook, you would have seen that there are a ton of great coding languages out there that you are able to work with. The more that you do your research, the more languages you are likely to find. There are many that are well-known and popular by hobbyists and programmers alike, but there are also some that have a very small niche that we are able to work with as well based on the kind of project that you would like to focus your attention on.

With all of these choices around to consider, you may be confused about which one to pick. But it is likely that when you were reading through the information above, you probably found that there was one or more language on the list that really spoke to you. Did one of them stand out as a good choice because it offered a lot of options, or would really help you work with some of the projects that you had in mind from the start?

Did you take a look at the language and notice that it had a syntax that seemed to click with you and made the most sense? Did you take a look at some of the resources that were out there for some of the different languages, and found that one had better resources or at least ones that spoke to you a bit more than the others, and that is why you would like to give it a try?

Even if you want to pick a language because it will help you to get further ahead in your own career and will make life easier, that is fine as well. Each person is going to have their own journey when it comes to working with a coding language, and you can start with one language over another for so many reasons along the way.

Take your time to do a bit of research before you get started. See what options are there, figure out which ones are the best for your needs, find the features, the benefits, and the negatives, and then compare the ones that seem the most interesting for you. It is possible for you to go through and learn more than one language as well, so if you find that there are a few of these coding languages hat you would like to work with, then you will be able to do that too. Through these steps, you will find that it is possible to learn the language that you want and pick out the one that is the best for your needs.

You Can Switch if You Want

Maybe you went through and tried out a new language. You were all excited about what you could do with it, you heard a lot of other people talking about this language and all that it is able to do to help us see some results, and you are ready to get going. You read up on some of the rules that were needed for this kind of language, and you are ready to take it on and go.

With this in mind, sometimes the language is not going to be the one that you are really liking at the time. Sure, you were excited to get excited and see what would happen, but now that you are in it, you are not feeling it. Maybe it is not working the way that you want. Maybe it is harder than you would like to work with. Or maybe you find that it is not going to help you reach some of your goals and is just not working for the specific application that you have.

This is a completely normal feeling. You do not have to stick with a coding language just because you started out with it. You do need to consider why you want to stop ahead of time though. If you are just stopping because you don't want to actually try that hard or it didn't instantly become easy then even changing is not going to make a difference and you are going to end up with the same problem.

If you have given the coding language some time, and it is still not working the way that you would like, then it is time for you to consider a change. There are a lot of great coding languages out there, and many programmers start with a language, decide that it is not for them, and then switch over to the next one. And because they have some of the basics down from that first language, and they have a better idea of what they like and don't like with a coding language thanks to the experience, it is going to be a lot easier to work with the second coding language.

Before you go through and make those big changes to the coding language that you are working with, think about why you want to change. Did you actually spend your time giving it a good try? Have you been learning, asking for help, and trying out a lot of different things, and it still is not matching up the way that you would like? Have you found out that there is another language that would help you to reach your career goals better than this one? Or are you just not motivating yourself and sticking with it the way that you should get the results that you are looking for.

Taking a deep look at yourself and what is going on is important. This is the only way that you will be able to make sure that you are actually changing because it is the best thing for you, and will keep you going on the right path to seeing the results that you would like.

Is There One for a Particular Field?

Many people decide that it is in their best interests to learn how to code because it would provide them with some more career opportunities than any other thing. With many of the professional and even technical jobs that are out there, we will find that knowing how to work with a coding language can be a good way for us to get our foot in the door.

Many times this could be the thing that sets you apart from some of the other candidates for the position. In fact, sometimes the position may not need coding in the first place, but it could be useful for a future project that the company would like to work with, and will help you to stand out as a good person for the job.

Then there are those jobs that specifically need some of the codings to help them be successful, and you will need to make sure that you know one or more coding languages in order to even be considered for the position. If you want to get that position, you will need to make sure that you know some of the coding languages that they require, at least the beginnings of it, and then learn from there and grow your knowledge over time.

For some positions, just having the experience and knowing some kind of coding language is going to be enough. This gives you some freedom because you are able to just show that you do know a coding language along the way, and then if there are some specific changes that they need later on. Then there are some positions that will require a certain type of coding language, and then you need to make sure that you are learning the right language in order to further your own career along the way.

You will need to do the right kind of research ahead of time in order to get started with this. Sometimes the coding will be listed out specifically in the job description that you would like to work with. Other times you would have to just know enough about the industry and can pick the languages that are the most common from there.

Once you have information about the kinds of coding languages, it is time to start learning about them as you do your job searching. The basics can often help us to get going, but you will find that the more that you are able to work with and learn about the specific language that you need for that job, the more of a hot commodity you will be for the job that you are trying to apply for along the way as well.

Another cool thing is that it is going to be pretty easy for you to learn more than one language when you would like. Once you have some of the basics down from this guidebook, as well as some of the basics from that first coding language that you wanted to learn, then you will find that the second, the third, and even the fourth language will be easier.

Due to the fact that so many of these languages are going to share a lot of features that are similar to one another, it is going to be easier to learn the subsequent languages that you would like once you have been able to get started. This is going to help make things easier for what you would like to accomplish and will ensure that you are going to see some great results in the process. So, if you find that you need to know more than one language for your chosen career, you will find that the hardest one is going to be the first, and then these languages will get easier from there.

There are so many great coding languages that awe are able to work with, and picking out the right one is going to be a hard decision. You have to take a look at how you are going to use and work with that language, which one has some of the features that you are hoping for, and more. When you have this kind of information, you will find that it is a lot easier to go through and see some of the results that you want in the process. Follow some of these tips, and you will be able to create some of the best programming languages for your needs in no time.

Conclusion

Thank you for making it through to the end of *Learn Coding*, let's hope it was informative and able to provide you with all of the tools you need to achieve your goals whatever they may be.

The next step is to start picking out which coding language you would like to work with. We have spent some time in this guidebook looking at some of the cool things that you are able to do with coding, and how all of this fits together to help us to really get some of the results that we want within the coding world. No matter what kind of coding language you want to work with, you will find that there are a lot of o similarities between them, and once you learn a bit about one of the languages, you are able to use this to propel you into the future on a few of the others as well. But first, you have to pick out which of the languages is your favorite and which one you would like to spend some of your time on as well.

There are so many topics that we are able to bring up when it comes to the world of programming and being able to handle them all, and really get down into them, is a sign of a true coder. Everyone is going to learn at their own pace, but if you are willing to put in the time and the work, you will find that it is possible to see some great results for your coding in the process.

We hope that this guidebook has provided you with some of the tools and tips that you need to get started.

The beginning of this guidebook was devoted to some of the basics that we need to know. We took a look at the different parts and terms that we need to know about programming in order to get it to work for our needs. Regardless of the type of programming language that we are going to work with, we need to make sure that we are learning these basic terms so we know what other people are talking about along the way as well.

Next, we moved on to some of the basic features that all of the coding languages are going to share. You may be surprised at how many similarities there are in all of these coding languages, and while there are some parts that may change based on the language, many of these are going to stay the same. This is why it is often easier to learn a second or a third coding language after you have had a chance to work with the first one.

We also are going to spend some time looking at the best coding languages out there for a beginner to learn all about. Each coding language is going to spend some time handling different complex computer problems, and there really are so many options when it comes to picking out the one that is right for your needs. When you are able to pick out the right one based on the things that they are able to do, you will find that coding can be easier than you think.

When you have had some time to learn the basics, it is then time to do a bit of preparation. Many beginners worry about how to even get started, but we went through and took a look at some of the steps that we are able to take in order to really make sure we are set up. We looked at the hardware, software, and more, and even took time to explore some of the free options that you are able to use, o ensure that you are not going to end up spending a ton of money just to get started and learning.

There are also a ton of code resources that we are able to rely on that will help us to get started with some of the work that we want to accomplish here. This fifth chapter took a look at some of the options that we are able to work with, and will ensure that we are able to really learn to code and find the method for our needs. Along with this route, we will look at some of the many ideas you should keep in mind, and the important tips and tricks, that will ensure that your coding is as successful as possible.

Then the final part of this chapter is going to spend some time looking at the basics of how to choose a coding language. We went through the general information that you need, and went more in-depth about some of the different terms, features, and parts of codes that you need no matter which coding language you are trying to work with, but we will finish with some of the things that you should consider before you pick out the coding language that you need. This is meant to make your decision process in coding, and more so much easier.

There are a lot of reasons why someone would want to learn how to do some coding for their own needs. Maybe you have an idea for a really cool application to go on your phone or even online. Maybe you would like to be able to create a website, work on a data science project, or handle some machine learning and artificial intelligence. Or maybe there is something else on your mind that will help see a benefit if we work with a good coding language and learn how to write our own codes.

Knowing some of the basics that come with coding, and all of the neat things that you are able to do with them without having to know specifically which coding language you would like to use in the beginning. There is so much that you can do with these, and having some of that foundational information down can make a world of difference in how successful you are going to be.

When you are ready to learn some of the basics that come with the world of programming and you want to make sure that your journey is going to get off on the right foot right from the beginning, then this is the guidebook for you. Even if you are not certain which language you would like to work with, make sure to check out this guidebook to get some ideas, and to learn some of the basics that will serve you well, no matter which language you choose to work with.

Finally, if you found this book useful in any way, a review on Amazon is always appreciated!

www.ingramcontent.com/pod-product-compliance
Lightning Source LLC
Chambersburg PA
CBHW071140050326
40690CB00008B/1514